THIS COLORING BOOK BELONG TO

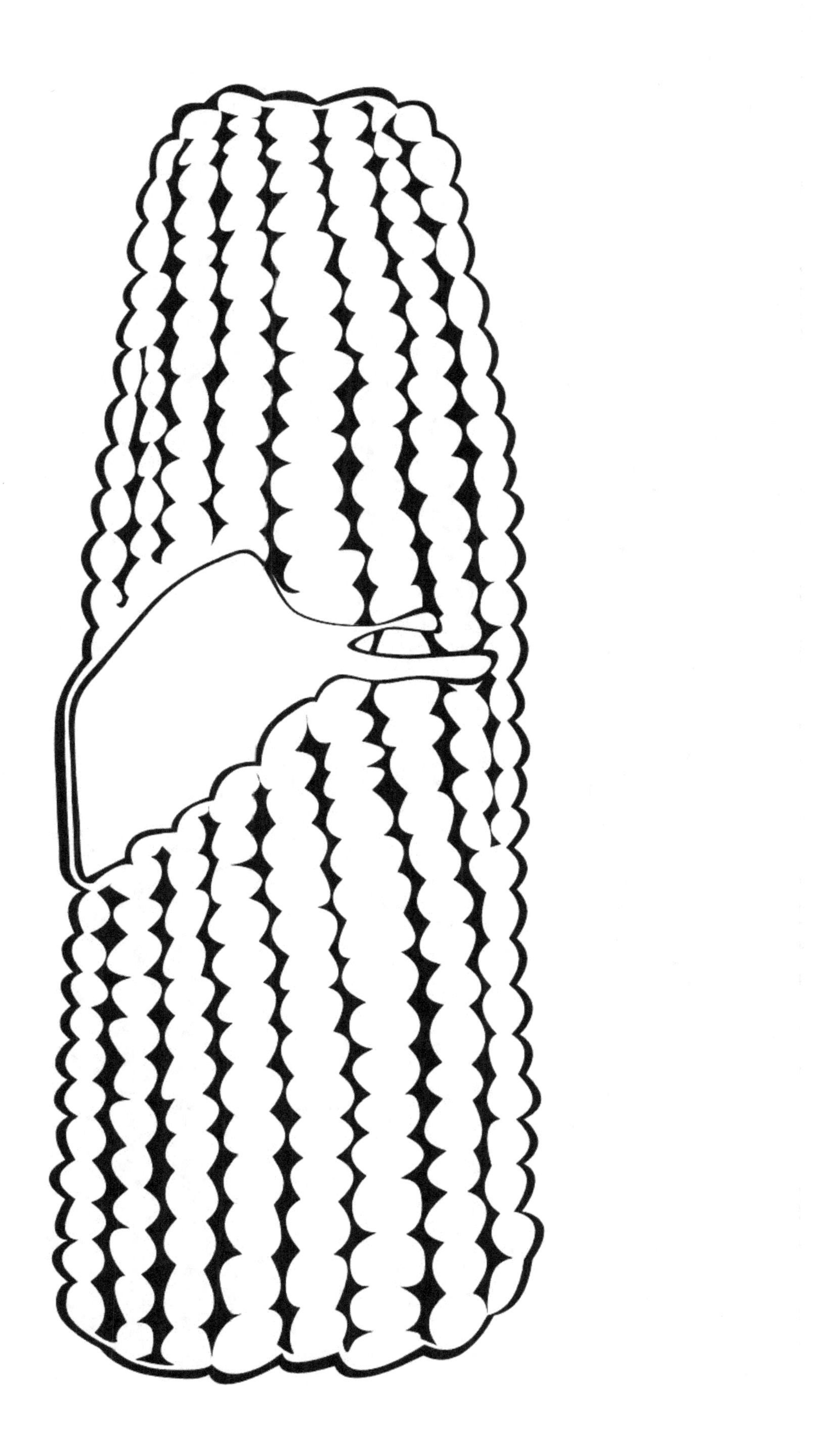

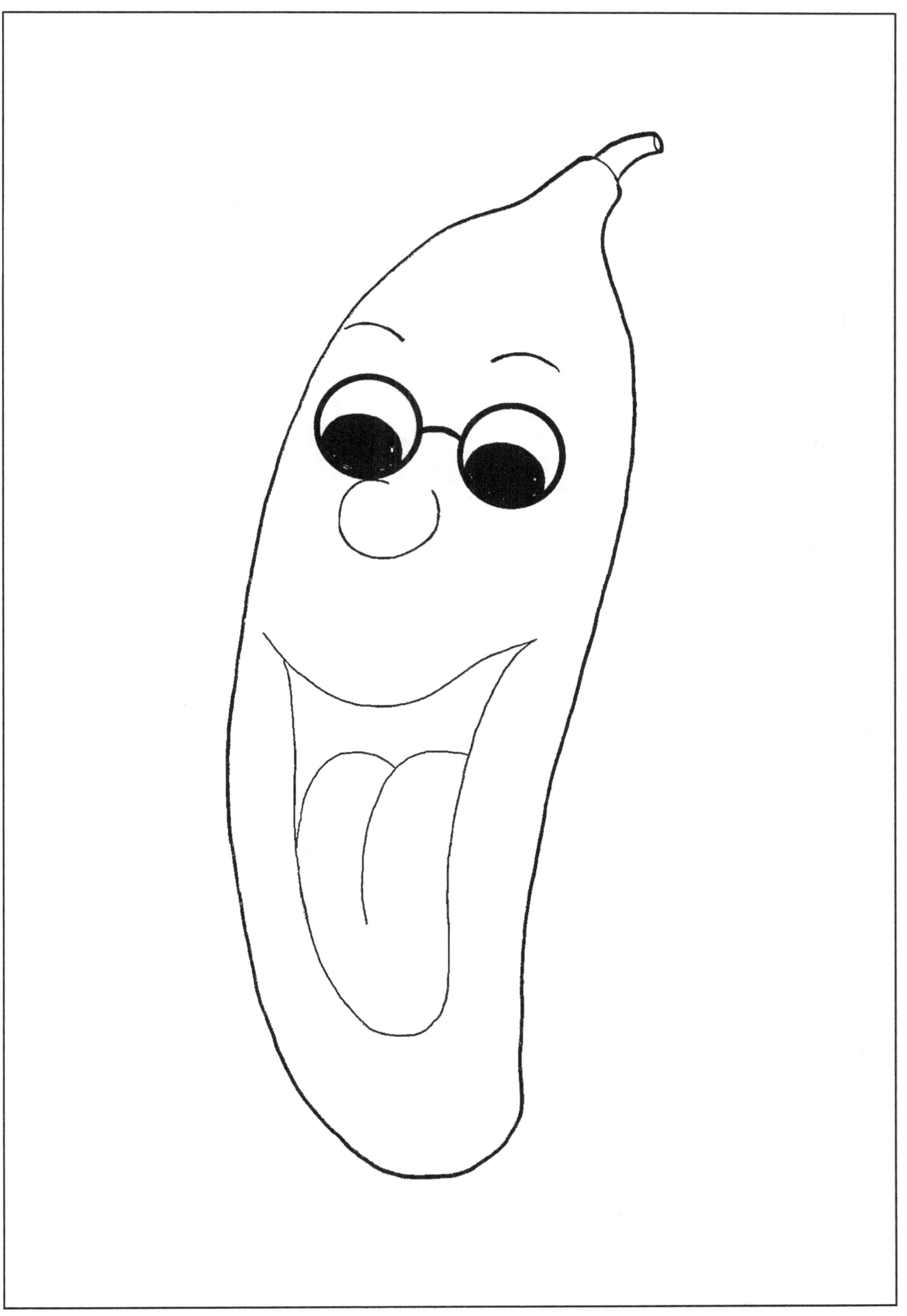

AVO CARDIO

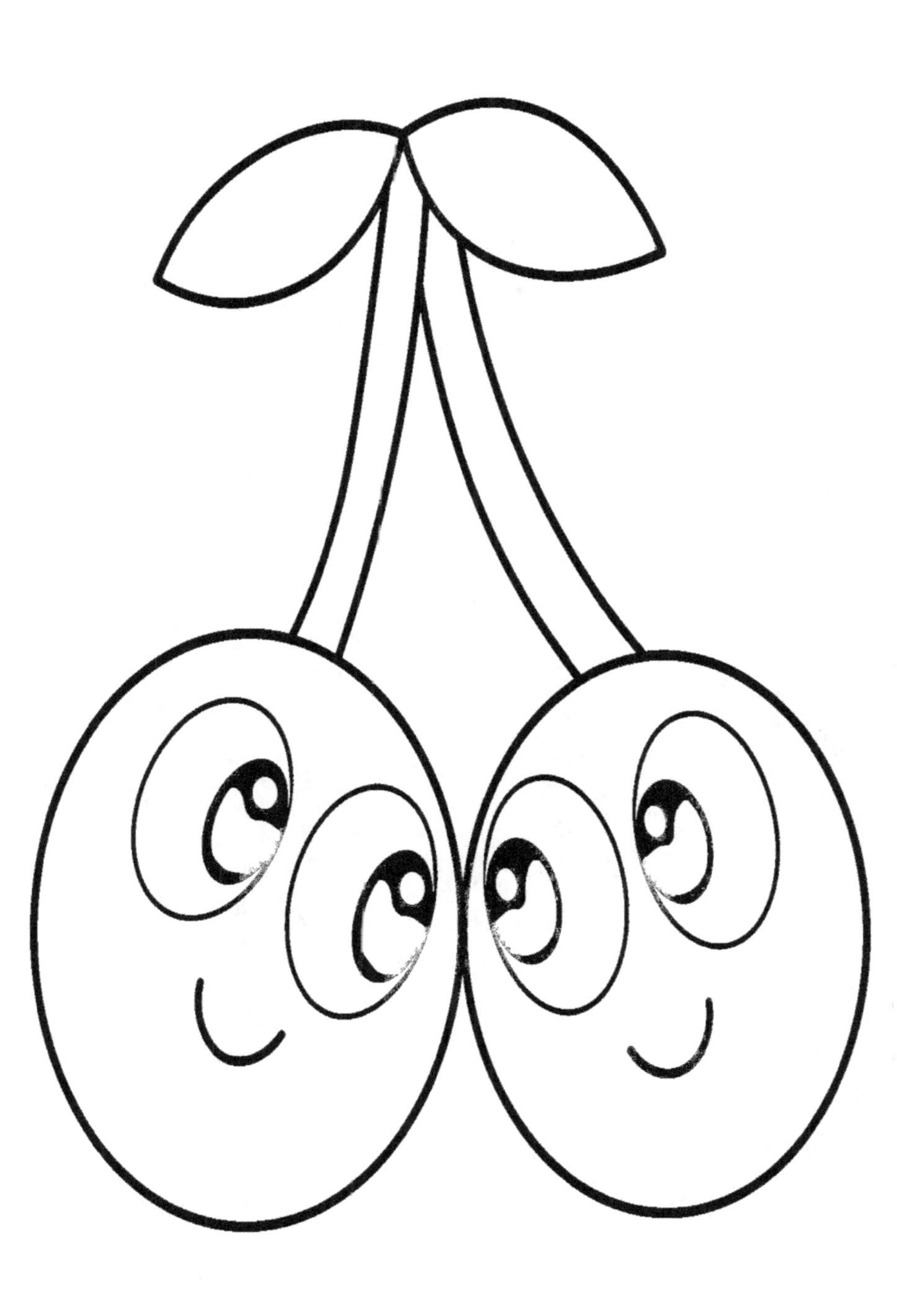

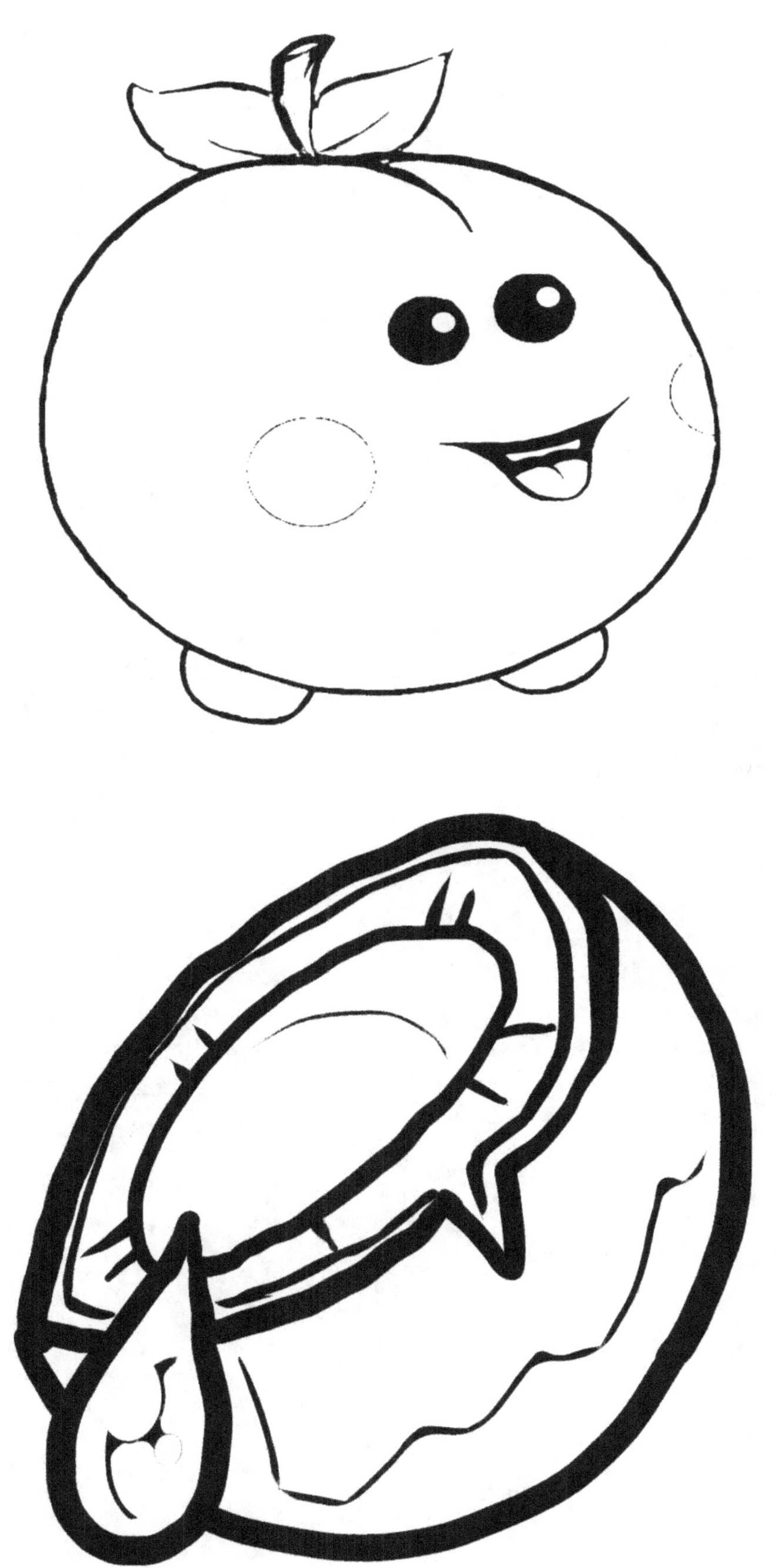

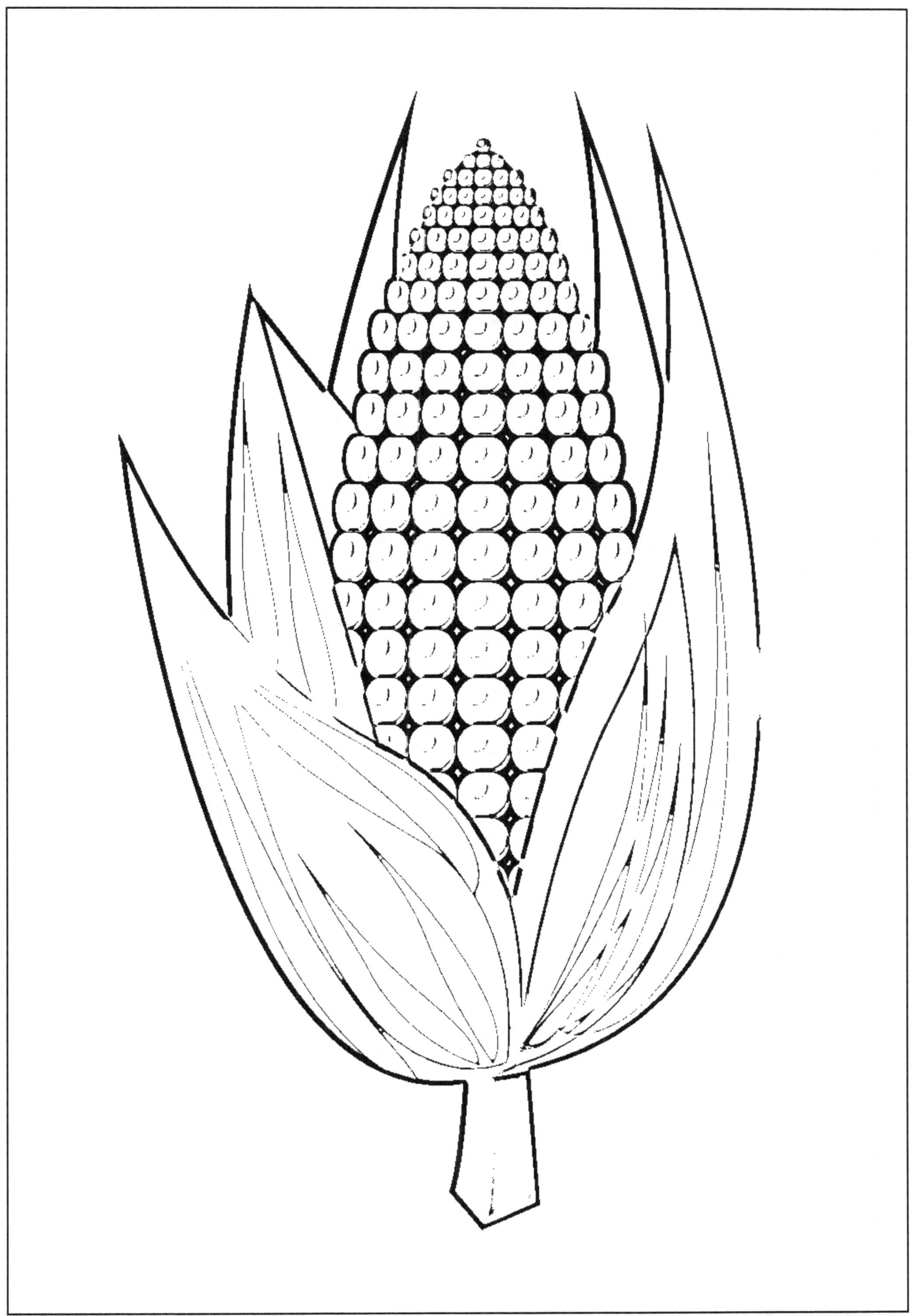

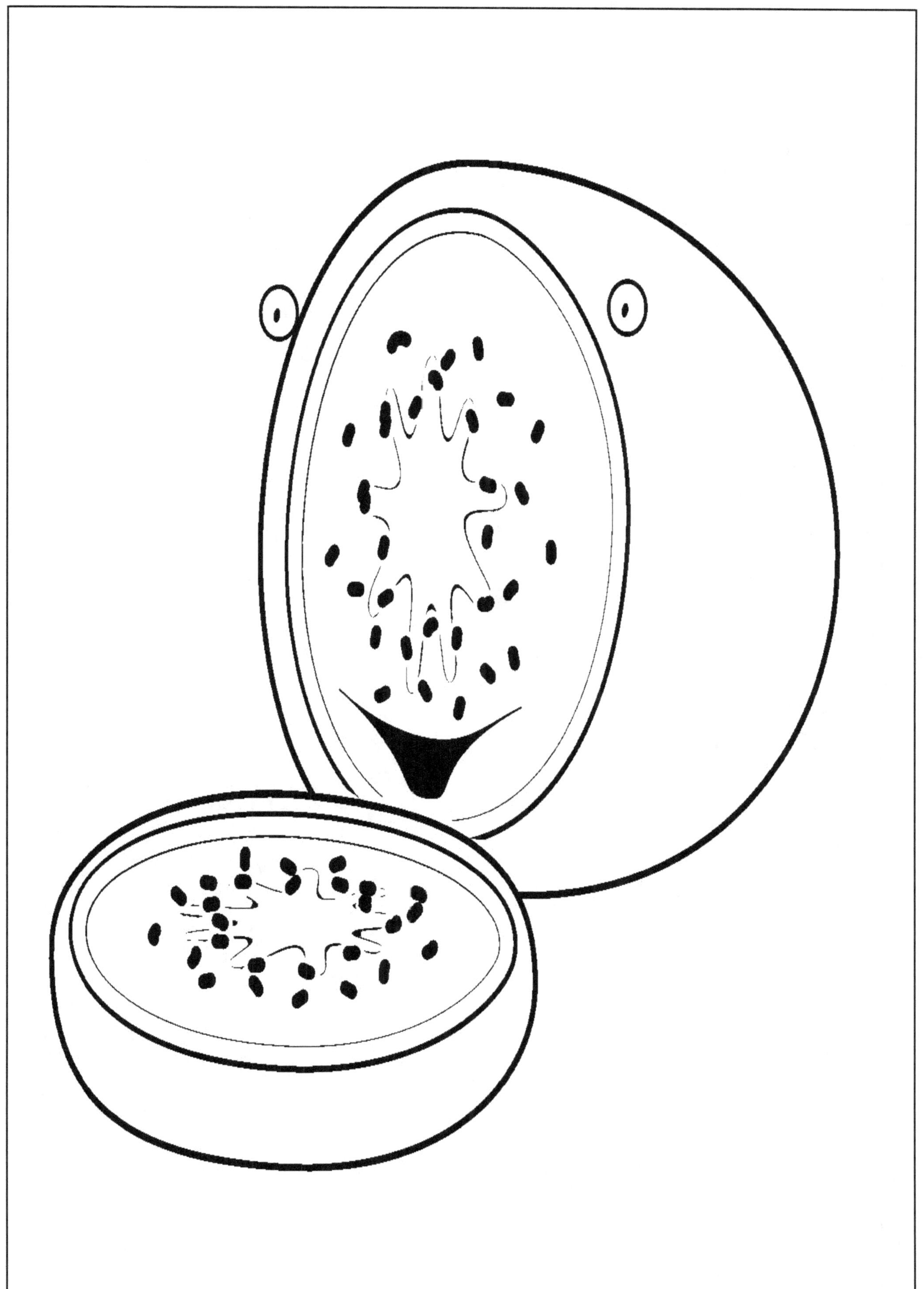

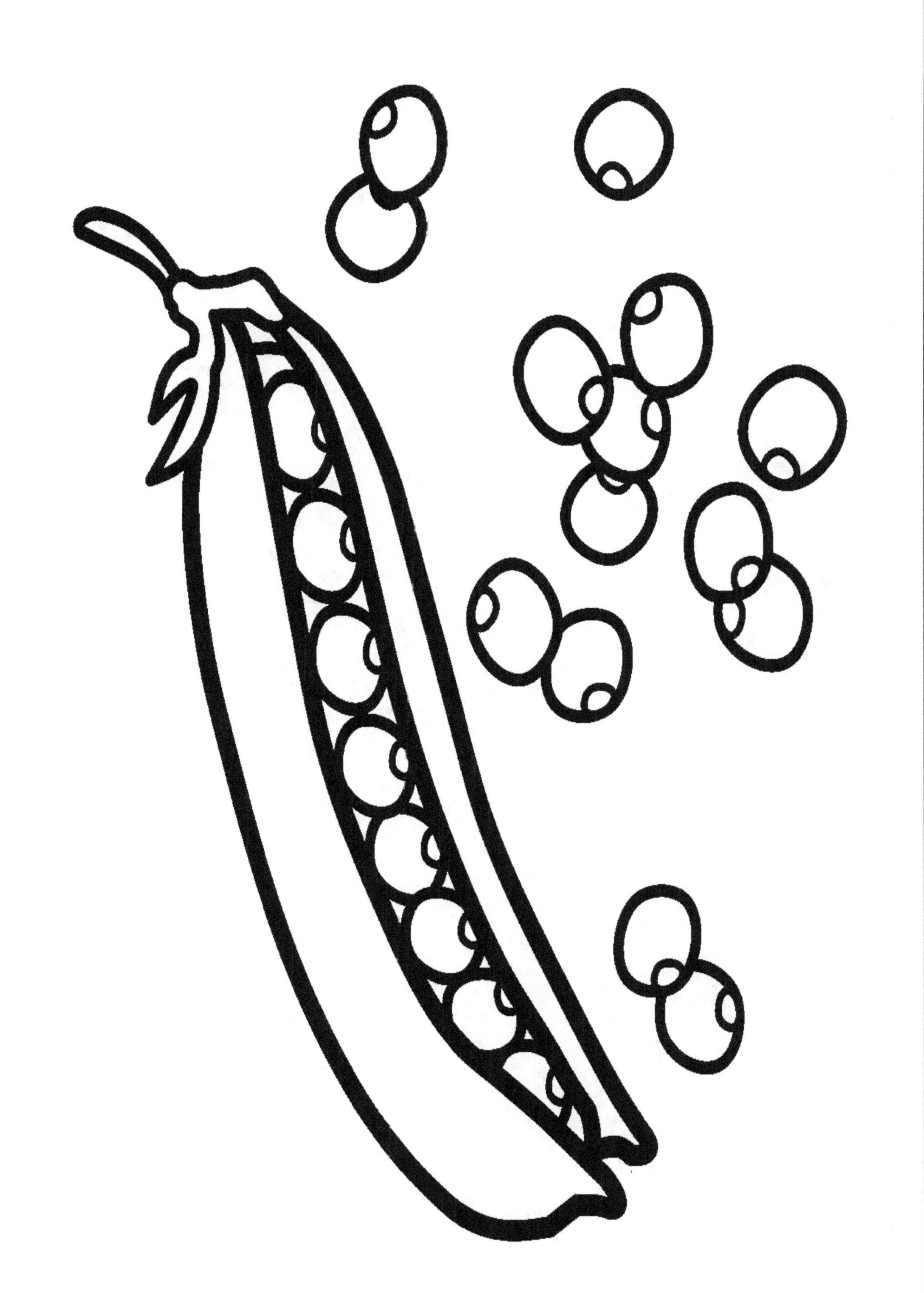

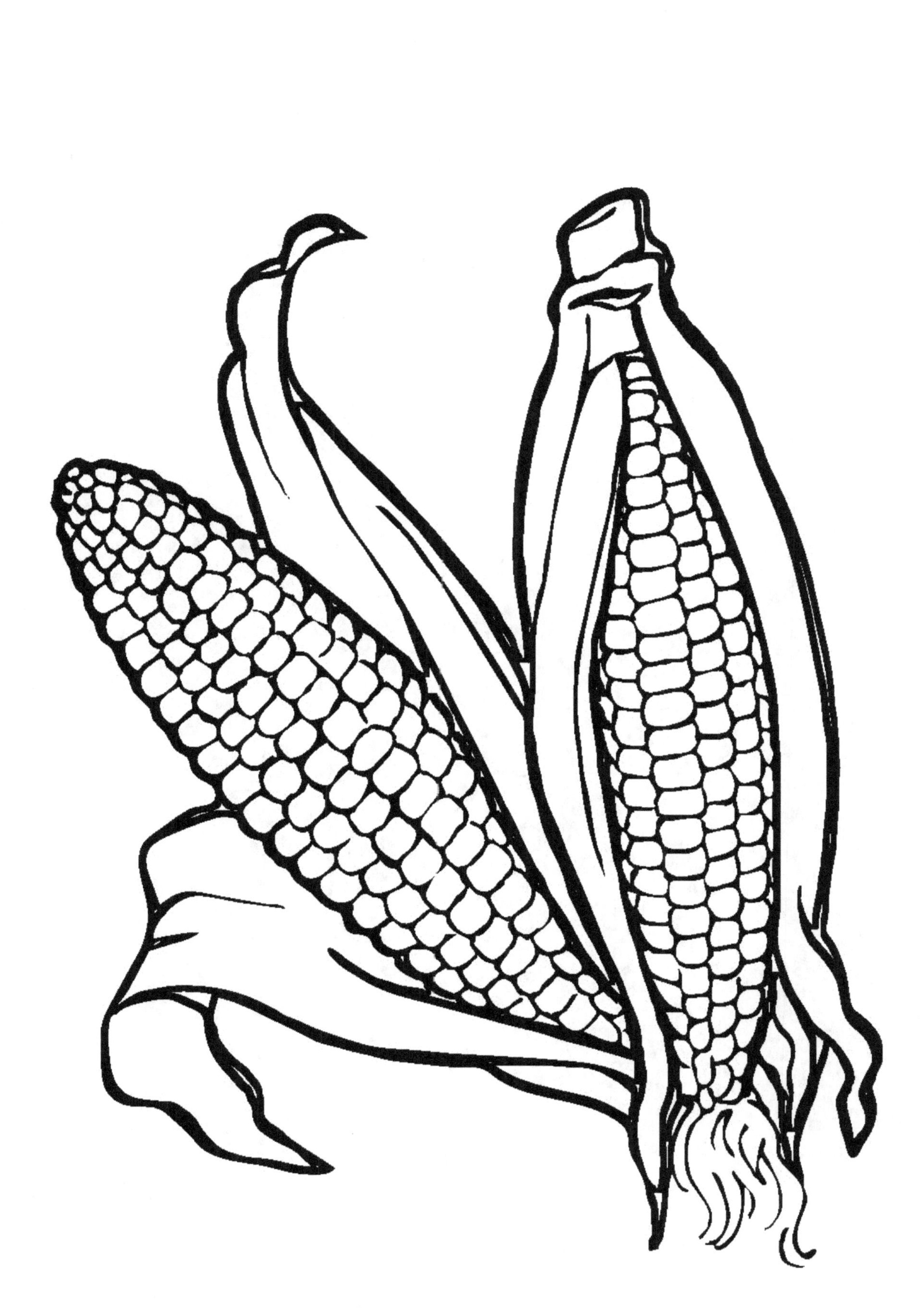

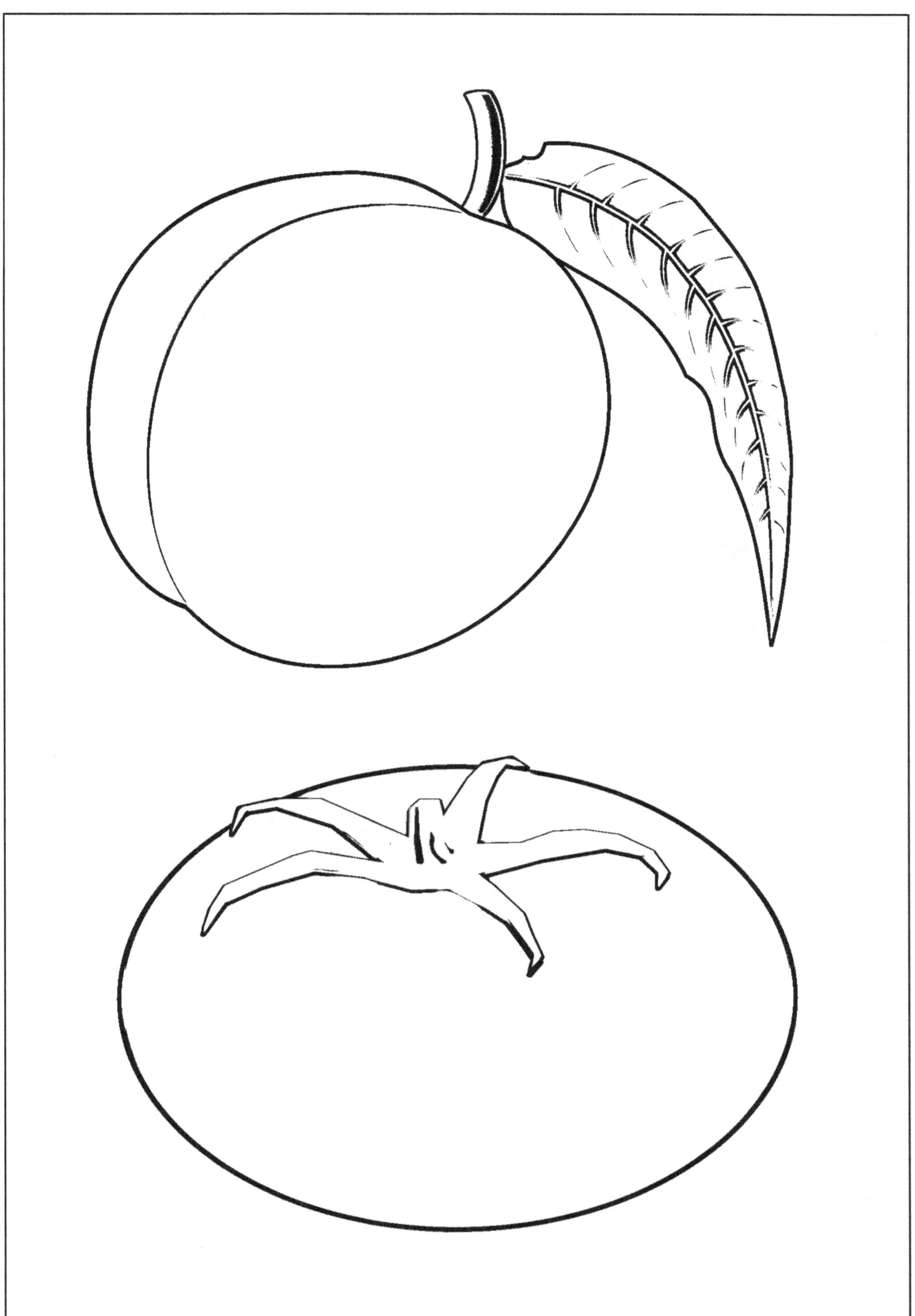

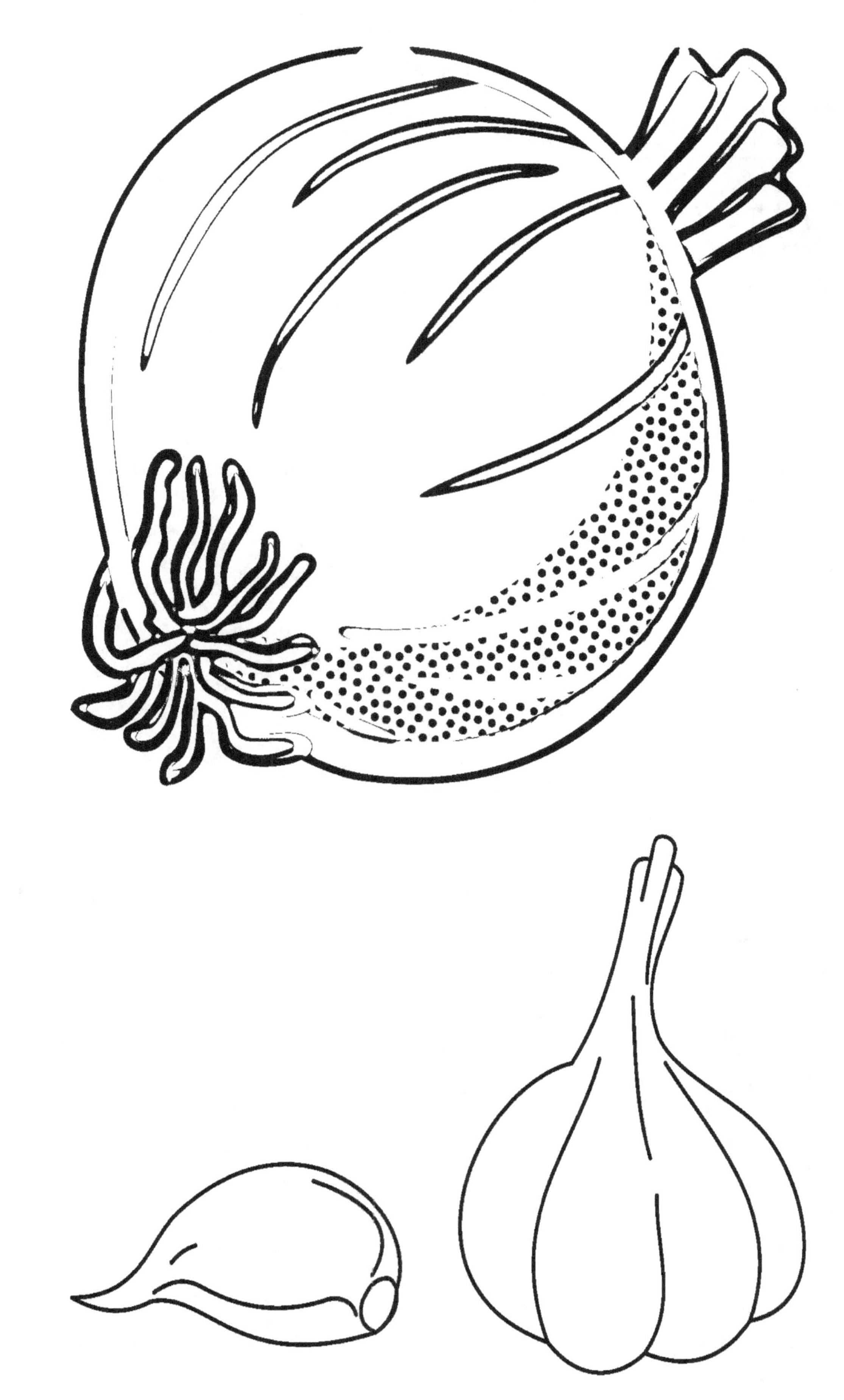

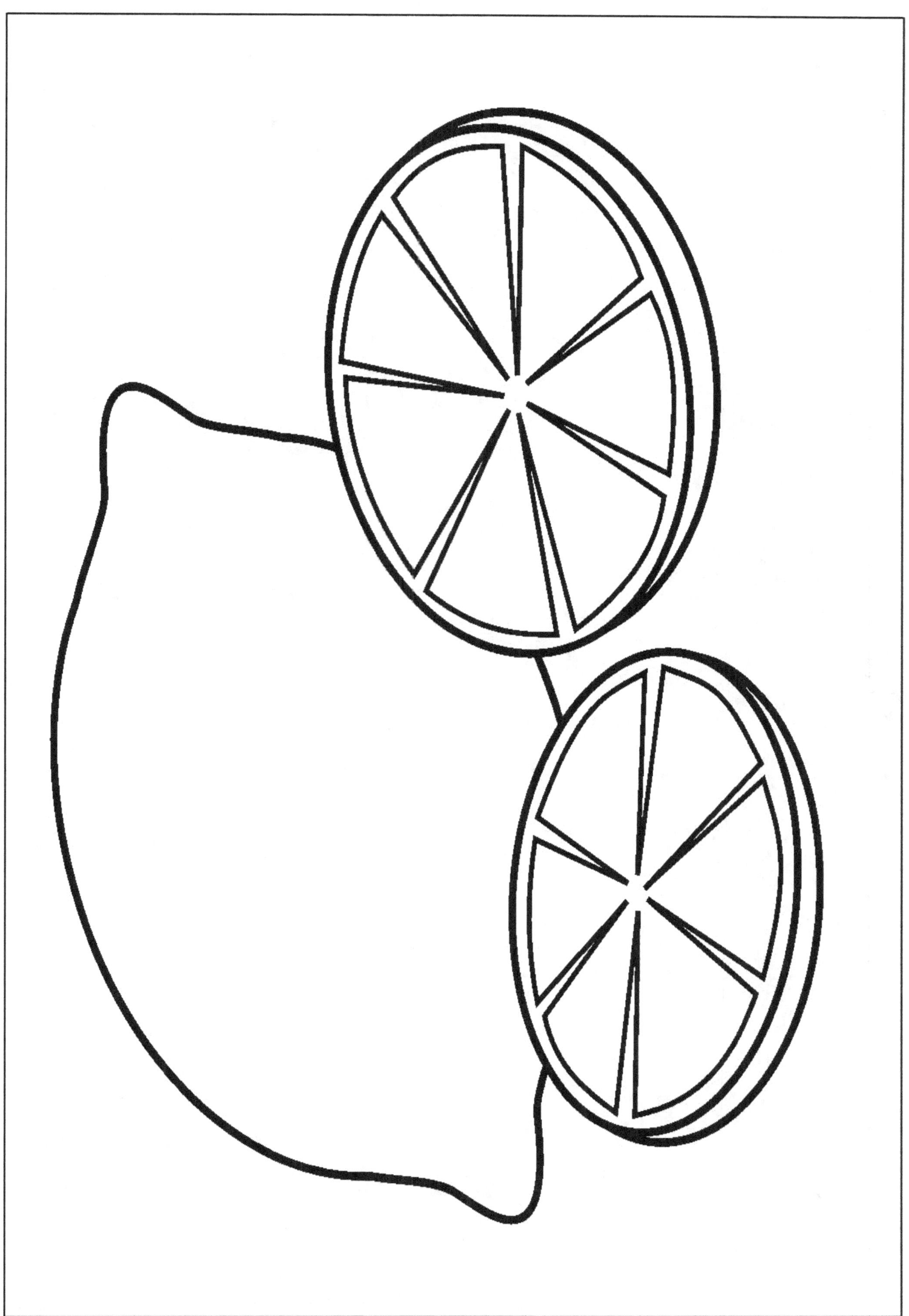

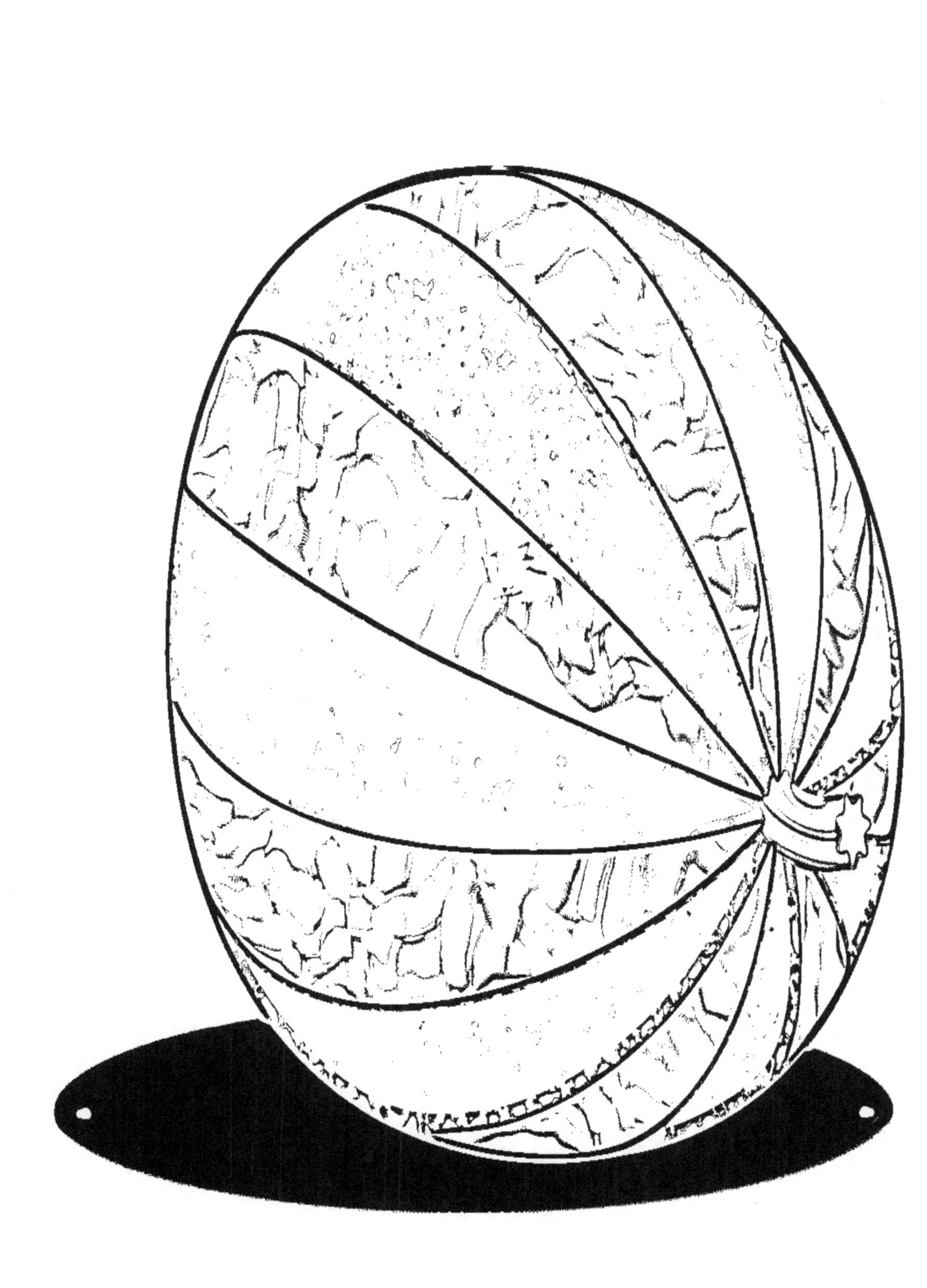

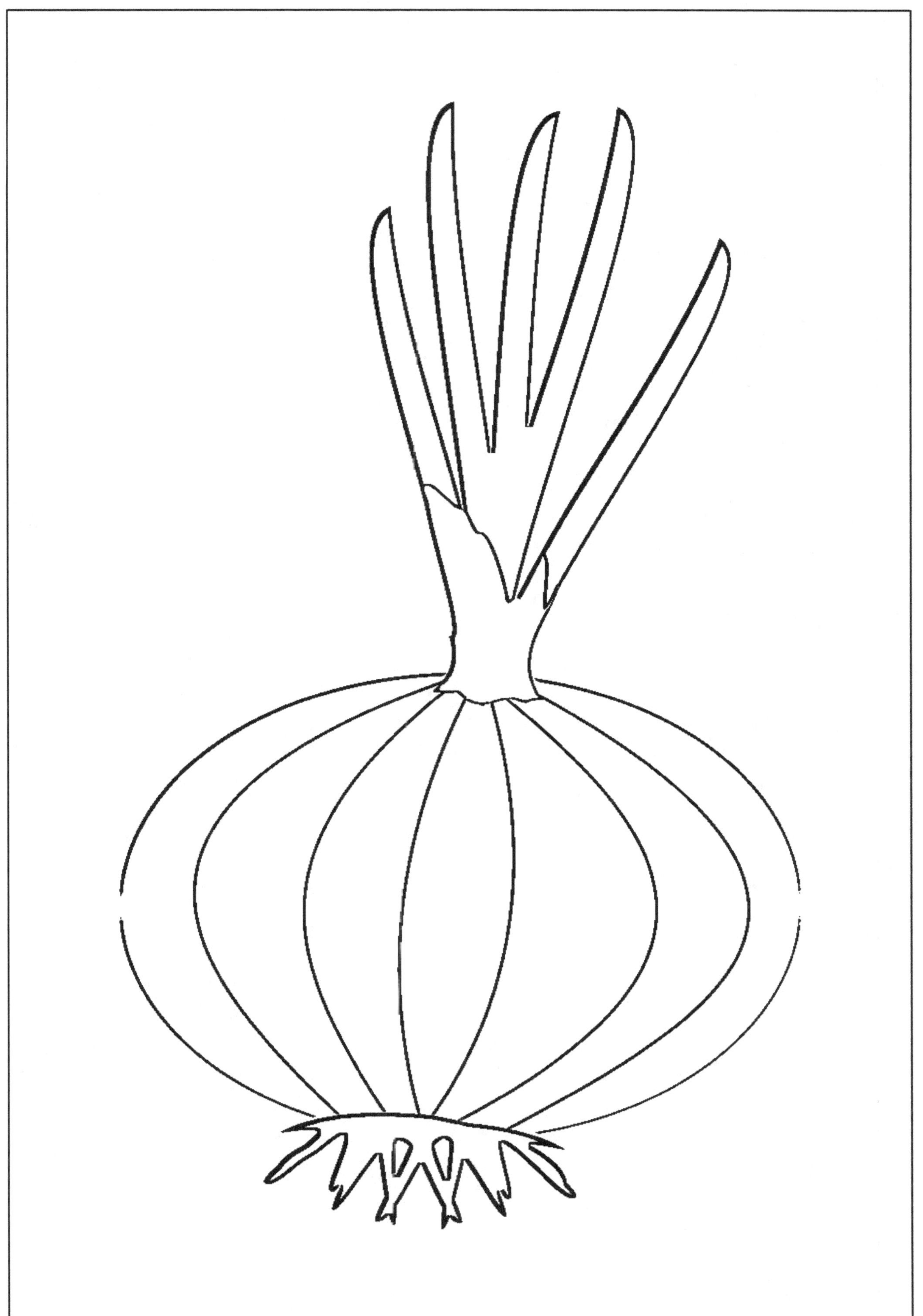

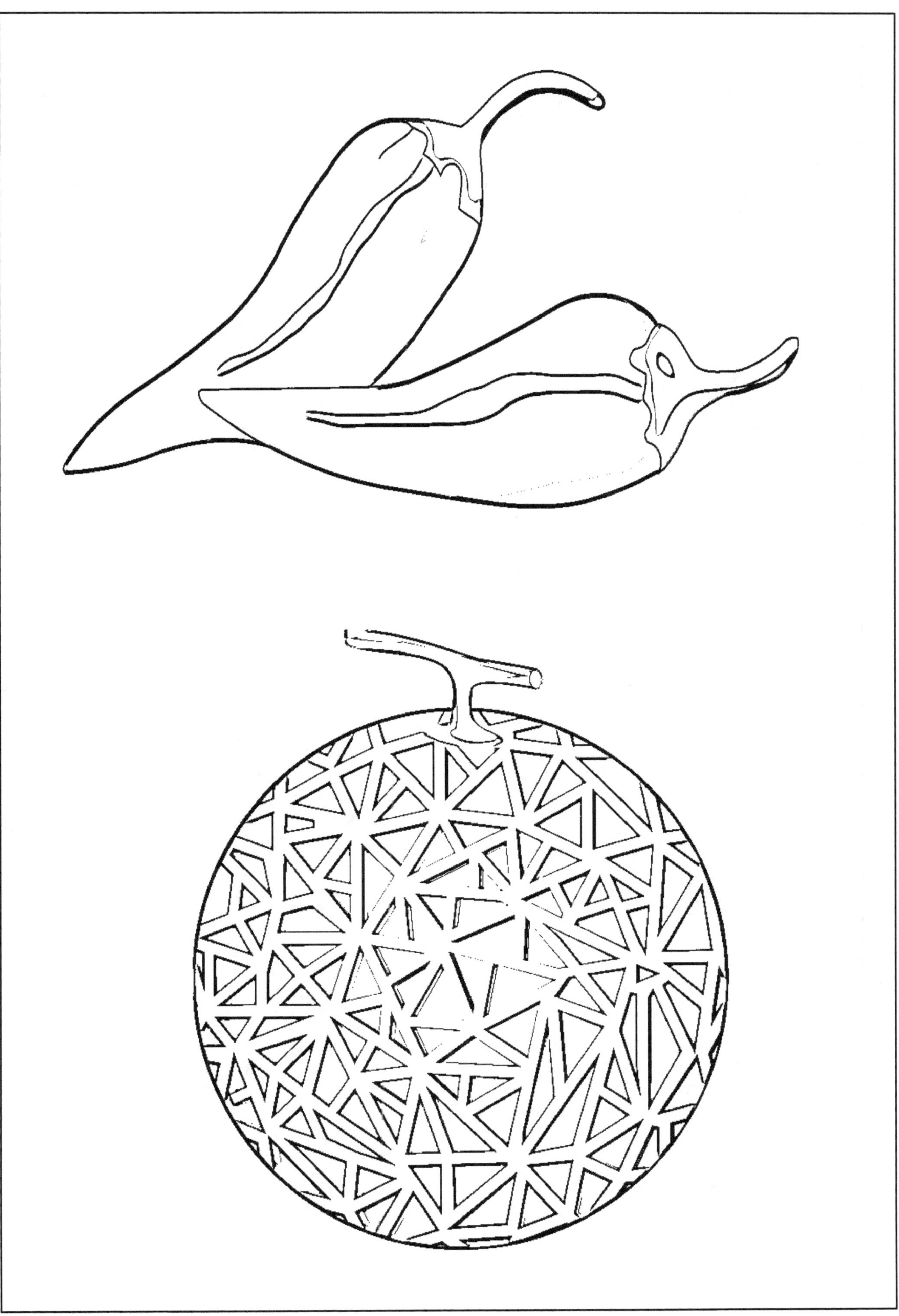

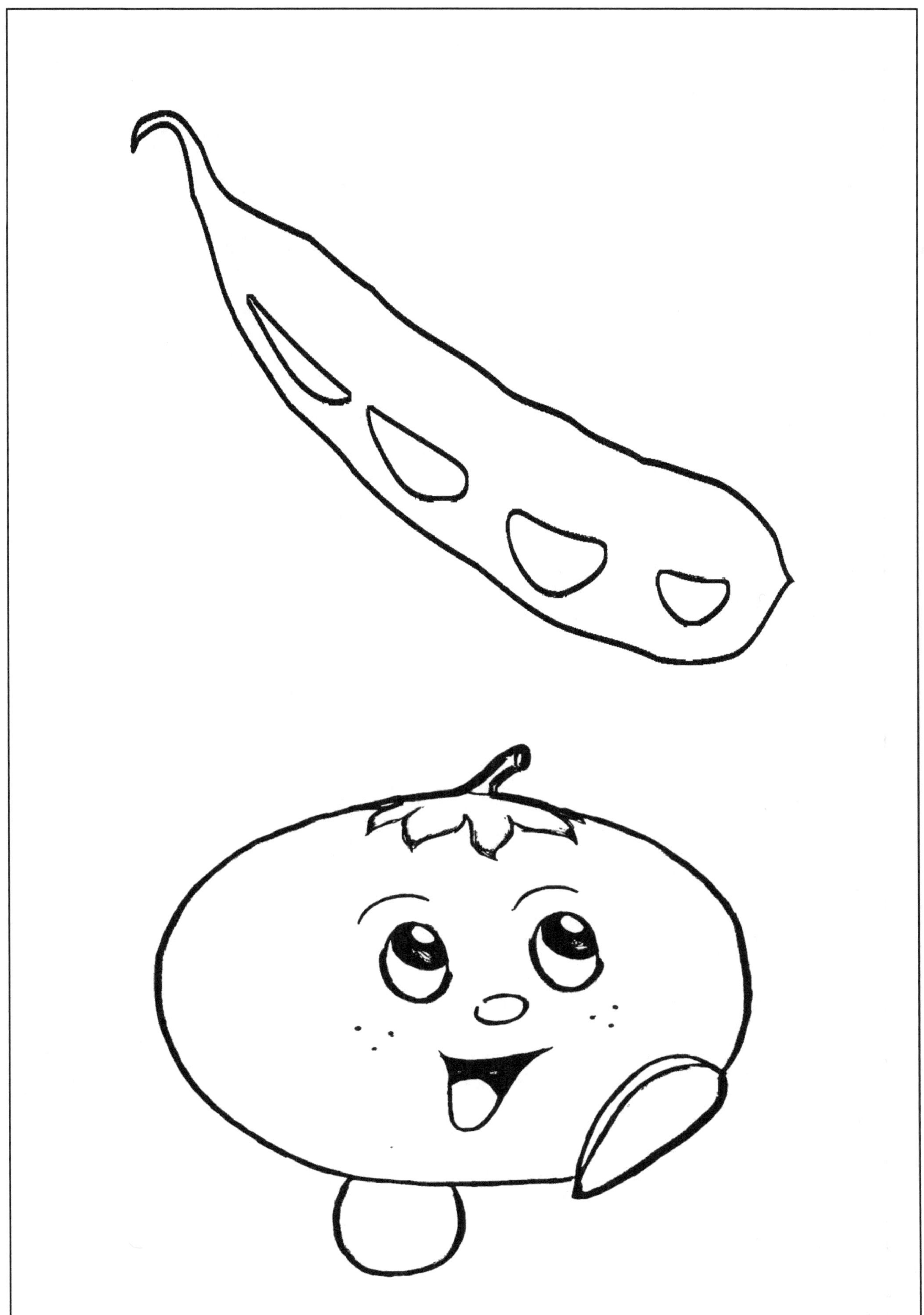